THE LIFE OF LESLIE JORDAN

A MEMOIR

DIANA PRESS

TABLE OF CONTENTS

INTRODUCTION

In the middle of the 1980s, when he was already in his thirties, actor, writer, and singer Leslie Jordan began his long career onscreen and onstage. He became known for his scene-stealing comic timing as well as a distinctive drawl from the state of Tennessee.

After making his debut in supporting roles in films and as a guest on television shows such as The Fall Guy and Murphy Brown, he swiftly won recurring roles in television series such as Boston Public, Hearts Afire, and Reasonable Doubts. However, his

performance as Beverley Leslie on Will &
Grace earned him the Emmy Award for
Best Guest Actor in a Comedy Series in
2006.

A commanding presence on both the stage
and in front of the camera, his little frame
conceals the immense skill that an actor
has. After receiving widespread praise for
his performance as *Brother Boy* in the
Sordid Lives play that was shown on
Broadway, Jordan would later go on to play
the same character in the movie version of
the play. As a result, he was able to launch
a fruitful career in front of the camera as a
character actor, appearing as a guest star

on a variety of television programs throughout the course of his career.

As a result of the consistent demand for his talents in the television industry in the 2010s, he made guest appearances on American Horror Story and **Living the Dream**. Early in the second decade of the twenty-first century, Jordan rose to fame on social media after posting a series of humorous and candid updates about his experience living in seclusion during the COVID-19 pandemic. At the age of 65, he released his first recording, titled Company's Comin' in 2021 - a compilation of vintage country, soul music, and gospel.

"CHILDHOOD"

Leslie Jordan was birthed in Chattanooga, Tennessee. Relating to a statement in 2014, Jordan said that his upbringing as a Southern Baptist presented many challenges for him. He underwent baptism 14 times in all - whenever the preacher would exclaim "Come forward, sinners!" the congregation would be compelled to respond.

Jordan also shared his thoughts on his personal life as well as his professional endeavors as he was a guest to Kathie Lee Gifford and Hoda Kotb in *Today*. He noted that his mother, Peggy Ann, was kind and tolerant of him, but that she never really grasped what he was going through. When questioned about his mother, he made the audience understand that she is a quiet lady who lives in Chattanooga and that she does not want attention.

When Jordan was 11 years old, his father, a lieutenant colonel in the United States Army, died away in an aircraft accident. Jordan's dad was a war veteran. Occasionally, things got a little rough. After seeing that the majority of their son's friends were females, his parents decided to enroll him in a summer camp for guys exclusively when he was six years old. They were shocked to hear that he had been recognized as the best all-around camper for his ability to make other people laugh. As is so often the case with LGBT children, he used humor as a defense strategy.

Furthermore, Jordan's upbringing in a very religious Baptist household forced him to confront the tension that existed between his values and his sexuality. At the age of 14, he confessed his drinking habit to the other students at his school and tasted alcohol for the first time. In 1982, Jordan relocated to Los Angeles, where he started abusing drugs and alcohol and was eventually got punished many times for his behavior.

When Jordan was 17 years old, he started writing in a notebook every day, which assisted him in his recovery from substance addiction and alcoholism. Later in 2010, Jordan shared with Wendy Williams, presenter of a talk show, that he had been clean and sober for thirteen years. Jordan revealed at the same event that had previously made him share a cell with Robert Downey Jr. When they subsequently starred in Ally McBeal together, Downey couldn't remember where they had met previously. But Jordan that he and Robert Downey Jr. had been cellmates before Jordan sobered up.

Also, work in Los Angeles came easily to Jordan because of his bubbly attitude, which landed him roles in a number of high-profile advertisements. He immediately immersed himself in the homosexual club culture in West Hollywood, and it was there that he began taking narcotics. It all began on the dancefloors, and then it just continued to spiral out of control until he was getting high at home and forgetting to leave the house. He developed into a fully functional addict.

Early on in the epidemic, Jordan became active with AIDS Project Los Angeles (APLA) as a partner and as a mobile food worker for Project Angel Food. Both of these activities took place in Los Angeles.

CAREER HIGHLIGHTS

Found a Peanut, which was performed on stage in 1986, was one of Jordan's first acting credits in the state of California. Other early roles for Jordan included a bit part in Richard Pryor's film Moving, which was released in 1988, and guest starring roles on television shows such as 1986 - The Fall Guy, 1987 - Summer Playhouse, and 1988 - Night Court.

In spite of the fact that he continued to get some tragic work on occasion, he realized that he was in more demand for comedy roles. And, in the year 1989, he appeared as a guest on episodes of the television shows Murphy Brown and Newhart. He also secured his first role as a regular on the Wes Craven comedy-fantasy series The People Next Door, which aired for just a few seasons. Thereafter, Jordan never took a vacation from television and continued to appear on the small screen in some form on an annual basis far into the 2020s.

Jordan also portrayed the part of the ski patrol director in the 1990 movie adaptation of the same name, which was titled Ski Patrol.

Talk of the 90s, in the television series **Reasonable Doubts**, he played the role of an assistant public defender; In the television series Lois & Clark, he portrayed the Invisible Man; He also appeared in approximately half of the episodes of the sitcom **Hearts Afire**. In the meanwhile, he also appeared in 1992 movies like **Hero** and **Goodbye Lover**, which was directed by Stephen Frears.

In the 2000s, he appeared in the television shows Boston Public, the Reba McEntire vehicle Reba, and Boston Legal. In 2006, Jordan was awarded an Emmy for her performance as Beverley Leslie on the successful series – having had a recurrent role on **Will & Grace** that lasted for years.

In 2010, his experiences as a homosexual Southern guy working in Hollywood were described in the one-man play Leslie Jordon: My Trip Down the Pink Carpet. A year later, he was a lead in the off-Broadway musical Lucky Guy.

In 2011, **The Help**, which was nominated for an Academy Award, as well as his lead part in Del Shores' adaptation of his own play Southern Baptist Sissies, were the highlights of his cinematic career during that decade.

In 2013, Jordan was given a role in the television series American Horror Story: Coven, which led to roles in the television series American Horror Story in 2016 and 2019.

On August 18, 2014, Jordan became a housemate for the fourteenth season of the British reality game program Celebrity Big Brother. This included him joining the cast of the show as a cast member. Jordan appeared in a total of two episodes of the British comedy Benidorm during the month of January 2015, playing the character Buck A. Roo.

The latest episode of the British television drama Living the Dream aired for the first time on November 1, 2017, and despite the fact that it was co-produced by Sky and Big Talk Productions, it was marketed as a Sky Original Production when it actually made its premiere.

Jordan's acting career extended more than 30 years; nevertheless, it was during the COVID-19 epidemic that he started attracting new audiences with his comedy and Southern drawl. His posts also discussed how he was adjusting to the changes in society - featured videos of himself, singing, dancing, and telling tales in his posts, which he shared with his 11 million followers across social media.

Having broadcasted a series of films on social media about the experience of staying inside during the COVID-19 epidemic, the actor, who was in his sixties at the time, achieved a degree of popularity without ever having to leave his house. This helped him gain a strong fan base.

Later on, Company's Comin', an album of gospel music, was published under his name in 2021. Afterward, Jordan appeared as a guest panelist on an episode of season six of The Masked Singer during

Week 5. During this episode, he also sang "This Little Light of Mine" while wearing the mask of Soft Serve.

The now-famous actor went on to play a single homosexual co-worker to Mayim Bialik's character Kat in the first episode of the Fox sitcom **Call Me Kat**, which aired in January 2021. During the course of the run of the series, as a recording artist, Jordan first presented his work with an album of cover songs titled Company's Comin', which included music from his youth. Jordan also remained active on social media during the length of the series.

After that, Jordan participated in the Academy of Country Music Awards as a presenter.

BEVERLEY LESLIE, THE ICONIC CHARACTER OF 'WILL & GRACE'

On **Will & Grace**, they had written this episode for Joan Collins. They had created this episode just for Joan Collins, in which her character, Karen Walker, was going to try to take Rosario away from Megan Mullally's character. They were going to have a "Dynasty" catfight and rip each other's wigs off in the process.

In the second season of "Will & Grace," Collins played the role of Helena Barnes, a member of Walker's social circle who was a competitor to Walker. However, when producers invited her to join an episode in Season Three, Jordan claimed Collins changed her mind at the last minute, despite the fact that she was initially enthused about the opportunity.

On the other hand, unknown to Jordan, the character had already been given the name Beverley Leslie - a small man with a southern in a white suit.

There was no way to dispute the fact that Jordan was the ideal candidate for the part, which was only scheduled to last for that one episode. Castanets in his mouth, he entered the room, and they didn't even bother to audition him.

After the first episode was filmed, Jordan's agent gave him a call and informed him that the comedy wanted him to appear in other episodes, including one in which Ellen DeGeneres had a role as a nun. Yeah, another one was completed sooner. And then he went on to take home the Emmy for best performance by an actor in a guest role in a comedic series.

Not only was Leslie a comic genius, and his back-and-forth with Megan Mullally was great, but the Southern flavor that he brought to the program provided a dimension that made it impossible to turn away from. Whenever he made an appearance in a show, he always managed to inject a little bit of Tennessee Williams into the proceedings.

The scene-stealer featured in a total of thirteen episodes of the program during its first run, which lasted from 1998 through 2006. When the program was restarted in 2017, Beverley Leslie was another cast member that came back. Before the series finale of "Will & Grace" aired in 2020, Jordan appeared in a total of four further episodes of the show.

THE FINALE

Here we saw Helena Barnes makes her debut in the second season episode titled "My Best Friend's Tush." Within Karen's social circle, she is known as an interior designer. Karen is a pill-popper and alcoholic. Joan Collins played the part of the person who stood in the way of Debra Messing's character, Grace, receiving a position. Therefore, Karen devised a strategy to be of assistance. Karen and the designer had the kind of passive-aggressive interaction that is common among so-called buddies. Keeping a secret is the last thing on her mind, despite the fact that she has an excellent one. Helena is a slob in addition to being pretentious and snobbish. She can be seen wolfing down tacos at a dingy eatery, completely oblivious to the fact that guacamole smeared on her face may make her lipstick seem sloppy. The attempt by Grace to use this strategy in order to acquire the job was unsuccessful, but this wasn't intended to be the end for Helena. Collins became well-known for her role in the television series Dynasty, in which she portrayed the sophisticated and cunning Alexis Colby. It seems like having her on Will & Grace would have been the ideal casting choice, but Collins didn't end up having that much screen time. A subsequent appearance may have resulted in a different outcome. According to what Leslie Jordan had to say about the episode, she did not find the screenplay to be funny.

AMERICAN HORROR STORY

The anthology series American Horror Story often reuses a significant number of its cast members from season to season.

Fans can't wait to see who their favorite regular actors will be portraying next, so this gives them something to look forward to while also allowing the performers to demonstrate their ability and versatility in a variety of settings.

Leslie Jordan became a memorable character on American Horror Story. He made his debut in the third season of the show, which was titled "Coven," and has since featured in two subsequent episodes.

Murphy only just confirmed the cast for season 10, despite the fact that the epidemic has caused several projects to be temporarily put on pause. Unfortunately, Jordan was not to be participating in the season that was postponed until 2021; nevertheless, this did not imply that he had not made his stamp on the program in some way. Jordan had a lot of skill when it came to comedy, and during the course of his career as both an actor and comedian, he played a lot of fascinating characters on the small screen. From the hysterical Beverly Leslie on NBC's smash hit program **Will & Grace** to memorable appearances on a number of other series, he had a long list of acting credits.

Some people in the United States, who are hunkering down because of the coronavirus outbreak, are turning to Jordan's Instagram account as a form of escapism during these extraordinary times. This is helping to grow the actor's reputation outside of his job on Murphy's long-running program. Jordan even mentioned the time he recorded a scene with the legendary Lady Gaga during the fourth season in a humorous behind-the-scenes image that he shared in one of his Instagram stories. Because the actor's sense of humor is reflected in the majority of Jordan's characters, his performances tend to provide comedic relief in the midst of otherwise terrifying situations.

AWARDS

The actor-comedian was honored with the GALECA: The Society of LGBTQ Entertainment Critics' Timeless Star award in 2021. This award is the Society's career accomplishment accolade, and it is presented to artists whose excellent career is defined by wisdom, character, and fun. The prize has similarly gone to Sir Ian McKellen, Angela Lansbury, John Waters, Fonda, Harvey Fierstein, Lily Tomlin, and Jane Meryl Streep before it was presented to Jordan in the Society's Dorian Awards film "Toast" TV special that same year.

SURVIVING WHO HE WAS – JORDAN'S PERSONAL STORY

At the time when the homosexual rights movement was beginning to gain momentum, Jordan was a teenager. In the late 1960s and early 1970s, as the American Psychiatric Association removed homosexual behavior from its own actual list of mental abnormalities, he was being confronted with his selfhood at the same time that ideas about sexuality were beginning to change in the U.S.

Then the AIDS pandemic struck the world. When the crisis was at its height in the late 1980s and into the 1990s, gay men like Jordan who were born between 1946 and 1964 and are hence referred to as baby boomers were the ones who were affected the most - By the year 1995, one-tenth of the 1.6 million homosexual males who were between the ages of 25 and 44 had passed away.

The failure of the Reagan era to respond effectively to the AIDS epidemic also played a role in this rise to prominence. Then in larger urban areas, the AIDS epidemic played a role in the rise to popularity of by now well-established LGBTQ ghettoes, which some hereinafter linked to *gayborhoods*. These districts, such as the Greenwich Village in NY and Castro in San Francisco, were the epicenter of the struggle for LGBTQ rights and the coordination of a vigorous health response within the community in response to the AIDS pandemic.

The political and social advantages of socialization among homosexual men - especially in gay areas - are extensive.

However, some studies have suggested that it may be connected with an increased risk of substance abuse. According to what Jordan said in a January 2021 interview he gave to, *People* he had a difficult time kicking his drinking when he initially moved to Los Angeles more than two decades ago. He confessed that the difficulties he had with drug usage were directly tied to his experience as a homosexual man living during those times.

It is particularly difficult for queer individuals who are less straight-presenting, like Jordan. This may offer people incentives to repress elements of their identity in order to avoid anti-LGBTQ prejudice and homophobia, which remains a persistent problem.

We've heard Jordan discussing his experience of having to play a straight guy in a cameo on Ellen DeGeneres' comedy, which created new ground in American society when DeGeneres' character publicly came out as gay in 1997. But even though he wasn't quite sure he could pull it off, he definitely gave it his best go nonetheless.

In the years that followed, he came to full terms with himself and acting, and played parts in which he performed the exact reverse of what he had done before. Because of the public nature of his homosexual identity, he served as a model for newer generations of LGBTQ individuals, inspiring them to come out of the closet and accept who they are. During that very same interview, Ellen DeGeneres also expressed her gratitude to Jordan for appearing on her program.

DEATH

After his automobile crashed into the side of a building near the intersection of Cahuenga Boulevard and Romaine Street in Hollywood on October 24, 2022, Jordan passed away. It was assumed that he had some kind of medical emergency that caused the accident. At the site, Jordan's death was confirmed by medical personnel.

THE FINAL SAYING

Actor Michael Jordan spent much of 2020 becoming an unexpected internet superstar. Thanks to his endearingly disorganized films, he gained millions of followers on Instagram.

Jordan's missives, which were shared on Instagram like clockwork during the day and were frequently captured barely an inch from his nose, were instantly empathetic when attention-hungry celebs started to spiral out of control at the beginning of the lockdown. He spent early lockup at a holiday home in Tennessee to be near his mother and twin sisters, and when he wasn't bickering with them, he was either slouched on his bed, trying to work out to Britney Spears bangers, or giving gossipy facts about celebs.

If you want to recall the life of Leslie Jordan by delving into his filmography, it's likely going to be difficult for you to decide where to begin. The actor, pioneer, and homosexual legend was stolen from us much too soon, and even though he could have easily had another 20 or more years of hilarious work left to accomplish, the list of movies and TV episodes in which he featured so far is amazing.

At this point, it's sure that many may be going to go back and rewatch their favorite moments starring Leslie Jordan, whether it be his time spent on **Will & Grace** playing Karen's adversary *Beverly Leslie*, his seasons on American Horror Story, his recent runs on the sitcoms *Call Me Kat* or even his performance in the drama film **The Help**.

Jordan, throughout the course of his career, took his over-gay sensibilities into the mainstream on a number of network series. Of course, many people saw Jordan as a symbol of the pleasure that comes with undeniably apparent queerness of reclaiming and finding delight in long-held prejudices about the feminine effects that gay men exhibit.

This has been a very demanding line of work. But he sure enjoyed the sudden popularity that came his way. In the past, he must have worried about keeping a series alive or pursuing movie jobs. But lately, he had not to worry about any of that. He did his best and was okay by the fans.

Does he feel as if he broke boundaries for homosexual performers in the industry? When you're in the middle of it, you don't see it that way, but when you look back on it, it's easy to see that he had a lot of courage to be so homosexual at such a young age. He claims that there were moments when others encouraged him to "take it down a notch" or "butch it up a bit," but he always kept true to himself, and that's how the walls were torn down.

Leslie's gifts of giving pleasure to everyone he touched, his ability to connect with people of all ages, and his friendliness, humility, and sweetness will be terribly missed by all.